THE GENESIS MEN,

NOAH & SONS

2ND BOOK
OF A GENESIS
BIBLE STUDY SERIES

THE GENESIS MEN, NOAH & SONS

Searching The Scriptures To Discover God's Truth

tjjohnson
www.hayneskid.com

AuthorHouse™
1663 Liberty Drive
Bloomington, IN 47403
www.authorhouse.com
Phone: 1-800-839-8640

Published by AuthorHouse   07/03/2012

ISBN: 978-1-4772-2868-5 (sc)
ISBN: 978-1-4772-2867-8 (e)

Any people depicted in stock imagery provided by Thinkstock are models, and such images are being used for illustrative purposes only.
Certain stock imagery © Thinkstock.

This book is printed on acid-free paper.

Because of the dynamic nature of the Internet, any web addresses or links contained in this book may have changed since publication and may no longer be valid. The views expressed in this work are solely those of the author and do not necessarily reflect the views of the publisher, and the publisher hereby disclaims any responsibility for them.

This book is dedicated to:

Those who have been faithful,

In Prayer,

and Service

To continue the work

Which God has equipped us to do

In our Everyday walk

With Him.

Those who offered

Gentle guidance,

Positive, constructive feedback,

and appreciative comments

That feed my confidence

And determination to write.

Thank You, and God Bless You.

~ CONTENTS ~

~ CONTENTS ~

~ GENEALOGY TABLES

~ GENEALOGY TABLES CONTINUED~

Finger Dancing

Words! At last! Here they are!
Pouring from obscure rivers
of thought; directing my fingers,
tapping gingerly, …then,
more assuredly they make words
Formerly lost…to me.

Words! Magically dancing,
Scaling the paleness of my canvas
like little ants,
leaving trails for their
Friends…to find.

Words! Full of life! Vigorously, excitedly,
Pull others like magnets. What?
Look at us now! A sentence,
a stanza, a poem, a prayer;
a chapter, a verse, a note,
a song, a melody,
A story…what a launch!

A tap dance, a key swag,
a letter mix, a word switch;
Three forward, one back, skip ahead,
double check,
Once more. Watch your ys
and your ts; your ns, and your bs;
Close to home, find they're
really not their own.
But my thoughts, and my fingers
Waltz the words…From within.

tjjohnson, 1998

~ Introduction ~

This book is number two in a series of Bible study guides that address the men of Genesis. The sub-theme is entitled *Searching The Scriptures To Discover God's Truth*. It is a continuation of book one, *The Genesis Men, Adam & Sons*. The questions are designed to help examine the whole word of God, including all the various nuances found throughout the Bible. Reading alone is not enough to fully understand the various meanings and the impact of each chapter or story situation. The Bible tells us to study the scriptures so that we may surely know, and not be ashamed of not knowing, (2 Tim 2:15).

There are twelve lessons in this book designed to cover twelve weeks or more of personal or group study. Let the Holy Spirit lead you as you use this book by tailoring it to fit your study needs.

Tools needed to fully understand Lesson Materials are:

A good Study Bible

Computer with Internet—not absolutely necessary but will greatly enhance your study resources

Bible dictionary and Concordance; some versions on line

Greek translation dictionary; can find online

Hebrew translation dictionary; can find online

**All Scripture references are taken from the
King James Version of the Holy Bible.**

Acknowledgements

I could not have finished writing this book without the insightful thoughts of my son Michael, who helps proofread my work and gives me significant feedback. I think mostly analytical; he thinks more subjectively. So a mix of our thoughts has been combined, and with the gentle leading, often nudging, of the Holy Spirit, this book is finally complete.

I praise my writers' group who reads and edits a lot of my writing. Often there was only one other person, William Harris, and myself, but we were two minds on a mission to bring God's Word to others who are spread as far and wide as our books will reach.

To all of my Bayview sisters and brothers who spoke a kind word of encouragement, just when I needed it most—I love you, and I thank you. I welcome the constructive feedback; and I am gratified that these Bible Lessons have been helpful, stimulating, and heartening. I am certainly optimistic about my assignment to search the scriptures and write what the Holy Spirit speaks to me.

And again, recognition and gratitude to my pastor, Timothy J. Winters, D.Min, who teaches the Word plainly to the flock that he shepherds, and to Sister Betty, his bride of thirty-something years, who is so giving of her time and support not only to Pastor Winters and the congregation at Bayview Baptist Church, but also to others who look to her for valued input and leadership.

Noah, Righteous with God

For Noah was not just a man,
He was a just man,
Mature, made righteous
and complete;
And he walked with God.

The LORD said to Noah—'Come,
You and all your family,
to live in the ark;
Because you, and only you
have I seen to be righteous,
In this entire generation.

'Gather seven of every clean animal—
Male and female,
Two of every unclean animal—
Male and female;
And bring seven each—male and female
of every bird.'
So Noah did all that the
LORD commanded him to do.

Then he and his family
went into the ark
To wait for the rain.

(from Genesis 6, & 7)

CHAPTER 1

~ A New Beginning, Part I ~
Noah

Background Reading: Genesis 7-8
Lesson Scriptures: Genesis 8:15-8:22

"And the LORD said unto Noah, Come thou and all thy house into the ark; for thee have I seen righteous before me in this generation. …and I will cause it to rain…and every living substance that I have made will I destroy from off the face of the earth." *(Genesis 7:1, 4, KJV).*

Noah was a descendant of Adam through Seth, the third son born to Adam and Eve. There were other sons and daughters of Adam and Eve besides Cain, Abel, and Seth, but they are not named, as is the pattern for many genealogies in the Bible, (Gen 4:25; 5:3-5).

Noah and his great-grandfather Enoch both shared a very distinguishing characteristic—they both walked in such a way that pleased God. Because of Enoch's dedicated and God-like ways, he did not see natural death—God took him. Because of Noah's righteous living, he found favor with God and was saved from the flood, along with his family. Noah's family was chosen to replenish the earth after the flood.

God warned Noah that the end of the earth at that time was drawing very near. In fact, God's said, "…The end of all flesh is come before me…and, behold, I will destroy them.…" Who was 'them' that God referred to? He said that he would destroy both man and beast, things that creep upon the earth, and the fowls of the air. God took into account the fact that every living thing, even the animals, and birds were no longer pleasing Him. He called everything corrupt, and said they were filled with violence.

Then the time came for God to activate his plan. I, for one, wonder how God felt about destroying his creation. The Bible says He was grieved with man's behavior, and God was sorry that He had made man. Of course we know from the Bible that God was aware of what He intended the earth to be, and how all things would be created, from before the foundation of the earth was ever laid. (Gen 1:1; Prov 16:4; Is 44:24; Acts 17:24; 2Cor 5:18; Eph 3:9; Col 1:13-20).

There was one man who pleased God very well. He was Noah, a just man who had found grace in the eyes of the LORD. So God determined Noah and his family were perfect for his plan. They became God's choices to preserve a remnant of humanity.

God gave Noah directions on exactly what he must do. Noah believed God. Long before there was even a hint of rain, Noah and his sons began God's project of building the gigantic boat that would transport Noah and his family to safety. When God decided it was time. Not only was Noah's family to be spared, but God included a male and female specimen of every living thing on earth at that time. Noah was six hundred years old when he and his family entered the ark. They would sail upon the flood-waters for more than a year before setting their feet on dry land again.

Maiden Voyage!
Genesis 7:6-7; 8:15-19

1.   Name the people of Noah's family who boarded the boat they had constructed by following the specifications they'd been given.

2.   According to the background reading, which month did Noah and his family enter the ark? Which month did they leave the ark? Explain the names of these months.

3.   Discuss the instructions God gave these pioneering sailors.

4.   Noah and his traveling entourage were on the water for a long time. Calculate how long it was before they embarked on dry land again.

5.   There was an entourage who disembarked from the ark. Name them.

6.   This passage doesn't mention the aquatic creatures. What do you think happened with them?

Dry Land—Sacrifices Offered:
Genesis 8:20-22
7a.   Noah did something very important when he reached dry land. Describe his actions.

7b.   How and why did Noah's burnt offerings please the LORD?

8a.   Discuss the significance of these offerings that Noah offered to the LORD. Give scripture references.

8b.   How could Noah dare sacrifice any animal that God had entrusted to him? How would he choose?

9.   Discuss God's declaration for man at this point.

The Earth Replenished—After

And,

God blessed Noah

And his sons, and said

Be fruitful,

And multiply,

And replenish

The earth.

(Genesis 9:1)

CHAPTER 2

~ A New Beginning, Part II ~
Noah

Background Reading: Genesis 7-8
Lesson Scriptures: Genesis 9:1-9:22

'And the fear of you and the dread of you shall be upon every beast of the earth, and upon every fowl of the air, upon all that moveth [upon] the earth, and upon all the fishes of the sea; into your hand are they delivered. 2) Every moving thing that liveth shall be meat for you; even as the green herb have I given you all things.' (Gen 9:1-2, KJV)

Because Noah was righteous in the sight of God, so was his whole family. These were the chosen of their day. They were the only people saved from the forty-day flood waters that swallowed up the earth of Noah's day. God blessed Noah and his sons and gave them a serious assignment. Their orders were to be fruitful and multiply and bring forth abundantly, which essentially meant to produce as many children as possible.

And so, they followed God's commands and became the progenitors of all mankind.

Noah

What to Eat; What to Fear:
Genesis 9:1-7

1.   Noah's family was already highly favored of God, and had been blessed beyond all other humanity. What could God do to bless this family more than before?

2.   God declared that every beast, fowl, bird, water creature, and all that moved upon the earth shall fear man. So were man and beast equal before this point? Discuss, and give references.

3a.   God also told Noah everything that lived would be meat for him to eat. Was man not privileged to eat animal meat, or chicken, or duck, or pheasant before the flood? Give other references.

8

3b.   There was an exception about what man was permitted to eat. Explain. See also: Deuteronomy 12:15-16; Leviticus Chapter 11.

Sign Of A Covenant:
Genesis 9:8-19
4.   How was God's communication any different in these passages than at other times? (v8)

5a.   Explain the term <u>covenant</u> and its significance.

5b.   Discuss the terms of this covenant God made with Noah.

6.   What was the promise that God gave to all life forms in verse 11 and 12?

7.   When you hear of a flood destroying entire towns and scores of people, what are your thoughts?

8.   Relate a situation in your life where it's clear to see that God has given you a new beginning.

The Dilemma of The Grapes,
the Wine, and Noah

Noah had a vineyard,
and naturally Noah tested his
product to prove the
Taste and quality.

One day Noah's tasting was
so extensive… he was overcome
by the strength of the juice
Of his fruit.

Ham, a son of Noah, found him
Naked and inebriated.
So Ham went to find help
Of his brothers.

Now Shem and Japheth
walked backwards into Noah's tent
carrying something to
Cover their father.

They were very careful
So that they could avoid
Accidentally glimpsing the state of
Their father's undress.

(from Genesis 9:20-23)

~ YOUR THOUGHTS ~

CHAPTER 3

~ Son of Noah, Ham ~
Part I

Background and Lesson Scriptures; Gen 5:28-32
Genesis 5:28-32; 9; 10:1-10

"Now these [are] the generations of the sons of Noah, Shem, Ham, and Japheth: and unto them were sons born after the flood. (Genesis 10:1, KJV).

According to the word written in Acts 17:26, all nations of men, (and women), are made of one blood. That blood flows from Adam through Noah, to his sons, to each person living today. Noah's three sons were responsible for repopulating the earth after the historic flood destroyed every person except Noah and his family, (Genesis 7:13; 9:19).

Of Noah's sons, Shem appears to be the first born, as his name is always listed first when he and his brothers are mentioned, (Genesis 5:32; 6:10; 7:13, 9:18; 10:1; & 1 Chronicles 1:4). There are differences of opinions among Bible commentators and scholars about which son was the older. Genesis 10:21 confuses the issue because it can be interpreted to mean that Japheth is the older.

We cannot always conclude that the first son mentioned is the eldest because the eldest son often does not have the prominent role in Biblical history. See examples concerning Jacob and Esau in Genesis 28:5; Joshua 24:4, and Hebrews 11:20. From Genesis 25:25-26, we know Jacob was the younger twin. In the case of Noah's sons, Genesis 9:24 clearly states that Ham is younger, but, younger than whom—Shem or Japheth?

This chapter introduces the predicament which Ham found himself in that jeopardized the future of his son, Canaan. Because Ham was in the wrong place at the wrong time, he discovered an indiscretion of his father. Noah was not only overcome by his wine-tasting, he was uncovered and asleep. Whether Ham accidentally happened upon his father in this condition is not immediately known. And because of this incident, Ham called down God's punishment, not upon himself, but upon his son and his son's sons.

In charting Noah's genealogy, the bloodlines of these progenitors help to paint a clearer picture of our Biblical history. Further, history not only tells the story of our past, it also predicts the direction of our future. I'm a firm believer that we can't truly understand and embrace our future until we've come to terms with what went on before. So we follow the genealogy of Noah whose sons were responsible for replenishing human life after the flood. We are all part of that family.

Sons and Grandsons:
Genesis 10:6-8; also, Genealogy References
1.   Chart the descendants of Ham from the content of these verses.
Use this guide to aid you in completing the names.

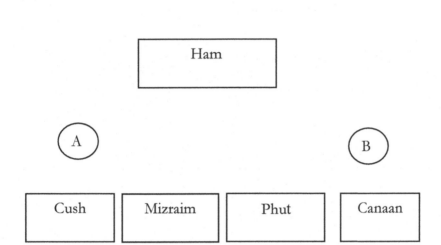

Noah

2.   Chart the grandsons of Cush:

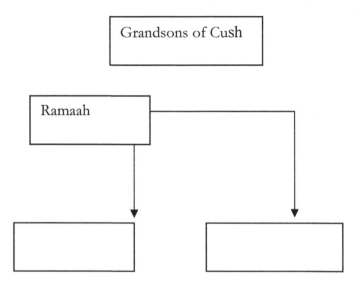

3.   Chart the translation, pronunciation, and meaning of the names of Ham's sons and grandsons.

4.   Indicate the cities that are associated with the names of Ham's descendants, along with the translation of each, (see genealogy references). Find a map that shows the location of these cities with regard to Old Testament location, names and locations for today.

Nimrod And His Kingdom:
Genesis 9:8-10

5a.   Take a closer look at Ham's grandson Nimrod. Research the actual meaning of his name?

5b.   Nimrod's name was associated with several cities. What city was the beginning of his kingdom?

5c.   Discuss the naming of city.

6a.   .It is said that Nimrod was a mighty hunter. Exactly what did Nimrod hunt?

6b.   Was Nimrod actually a king? Discuss.

Babel:
Genesis 10:10
7.　　　There was another name for the city referred to in question (5b). What is it? Give an example of what happened there.

8.　　　What is the translation of <u>Shinar</u>? Where is it located?

9.　　　Is there anything of interest that you discovered in researching the names of the cities that Nimrod built? What about their locations?

~ YOUR THOUGHTS ~

CHAPTER 4

~ Son of Noah, Ham ~
Part II

Background and Lesson Scriptures:
Genesis 10:11-20; 1 Chronicles 1:8-15

"And the sons of Ham; Cush, and Mizraim, and Phut, and Canaan," (Genesis 10: 6; KJV)

In looking at Ham's descendants and the interpretation of their names and of the names of the cities they inhabited, we can deduce that Ham's descendants lived in the south country. Psalm 105:23, 27 tells us that Egypt, *which is south of Canaan*, was the land of Ham.

Ham's name is interpreted as <u>hot</u>. It is said to be the collective name of all Egyptians.[1] Khen, an Egyptian god, is the Egyptian equivalent for the Hebrew word <u>Ham</u>.[2] The information of Genesis 10:6-20, indicates location as South and Central Arabia, Egypt, the eastern shores of the Mediterranean, and the east coast of Africa. (See map in Appendix A).

Ham's son Mitsrayim (Mizraim) was given a name that translated as Egypt—land of the Copts.[3]   Ham's son Canaan was predestined to forfeit the land that was named after him to his cousins—the children of Shem: Abraham, Isaac, and Jacob and their generations after them.

A majority of Ham's people had ('ite or ites') attached to their family affiliation. As in Canaanites, Hittites, Jebusites, Amorites, Girgashites, Hivites, Arkites, Sinites, Arvadites, Zemarites, and Hamathites, (Genesis 10:16-19). In short, all Ham's descendants were called the Hamites, according to Halley's Bible Handbook.[4]

[1] http://www.blueletterbible.org

[2] Halley's Bible Handbook, Zondervan Publishing House, 1965, pg. 81

[3] http://www.blueletterbible.org

[4] Halley's Bible Handbook, Zondervan Publishing House, 1965, pg 81

Sons of Ham:
Read: Genesis 10:13-20

1a.   One translation of Mizraim (mits·rah'·yim) is 'land of the Copts'. What does this indicate about his name?

1b.   Where is this country associated with Mizraim's name located? What land does it border?

2.   Mizraim had a son named Ludim, pronounced (lü·dē'). What is the translation and meaning of his name? Note the Hebrew number association.

3a.   Which of Mizraim's sons was the father of the Philistine families? Discuss the translation of his name.

3b.   Where are the country borders of these people? Tell the importance of their borders.

4.   Discuss the borders of the Canaanite people? Find the territories of their cities and discuss.

5.   Verse 20 gives us another indication of how Canaan's families were categorized or divided. Discuss.

From Shinar To Nineveh:
Genesis 10:11-12
6.   Right in the middle of listing Ham's descendants and cities, we find two verses that pertain to one of Ham's nephews, (Gen 10:11-12). Research the ancestry of Asshur.

7.   What nationality is associated with Asshur? (Hint: Research meaning of his name. Note the Hebrew translation number association.)

More Relatives:
Genesis 10:21-22
8.   Again, there is a close association with descendants of Shem in the naming of these brothers' sons. Genesis 10:22 lists a son of Shem named Lud. Look up the translation and Hebrew number annotation of Lud. What do you find?

Comparative Genealogy:
Scripture: 1 Chronicles 1:8-16

9.   Perform an analysis of Cush descendants from 1 Chronicles 1:8-16 with those listed in Genesis 10. What differences or similarities do you find?

10.   In studying the descendants of Ham, discuss information that points to things you have not considered before? Discuss.

Ham's Legacy

And the sons of Ham—

Cush, Mizraim, Phut,

and Canaan.

And Canaan begat

Sidon, and Heth,

and the Jubusite,

and the Amorite,

and the Girgasite,

and the Hivite,

and the Arkite,

and the Sinite,

and the Arvadite,

and the Zemarite,

and the Hamathite.

(Genesis 10:6, 15-17)

~ YOUR THOUGHTS ~

CHAPTER 5

~ The Curse of Canaan ~
Part I

Background Reading: Genesis 9 - 10:6 -32
Lesson Scriptures: Genesis 9:18 - 27

"And Noah began to be an husbandman,....And he drank of the wine, and was drunken; and he was uncovered within his tent," (Genesis 9:20-21; KJV).

This lesson reviews the beginning of one brother's servitude, or one people's servitude to another. Canaan's descendants would serve their uncles Shem and Japheth, and their descendants, for the rest of their lives, (Genesis 9:26-27). The naming of this punishment was Noah's pronouncement of blessings upon one son, and his descendants, over another son. Here, the sin of the father is certainly demonstrated.

Noah's son Ham was the father of Canaan. It's amazing to me that God did not set the curse of Canaan in motion. Noah, Canaan's grandfather was. Even so, this curse was part of God's plan for Canaan, and like the curse of Adam and Eve in the garden—the consequences would echo from that time in history even to this day.

Canaan is the fourth listed, and possibly the youngest son of Ham. Why wasn't the first-born, or second-born son, or third-born son of Ham punished instead? We don't know. We have no indication of how this was determined. God's thoughts and ways are so superior to our thoughts—we are left wondering.

My curiosity is stirred. Did Noah fall into a drunken stupor in his tent while he was undressing? Did he leave the entry way wide open? Did Ham call out to his father, and hearing no response become alarmed, and decide to investigate why there was no answer? Did Ham already suspect that Noah had tested his crop's yield a little too heavily, and deciding to check on his father, come upon his father in that embarrassing situation? Too close to an open entry way?

If Noah left the tent entryway wide open for anyone to observe the inside, was Ham the first son to approach the tent to see if his father was okay? Did Ham's brothers realize just how much the wine had affected their father? Was Ham more concerned about his father than his brothers were?

All these are very interesting questions. The answers are not given in the text; however, we realize from what followed Ham's experience that seeing his father's nakedness warranted severe punishment on his behalf—cursing the future of his son Canaan.

A Husbandman:
Genesis 9:18-22
1.   Trace the family lines of Shem and Japheth. Draw a flowchart or delineate them in a table that clearly shows the relation of each, (see background references).

2.   Discuss the role of a <u>husbandman</u>?

3. Verse twenty-one simply tells us that Noah sampled the wine of his vineyard. This sampling resulted in Noah's inebriation as he lay uncovered in his tent. Discuss this situation.

Ham's Unfortunate Situation:
Genesis 22-25

4. Might Ham have accidentally come upon his father sleeping in a drunken state in his tent? Discuss.

5. Why do you think Ham told his two brothers about their father's condition rather than cover Noah himself?

6a. How could Ham have known that seeing his father's state of undress was such a terrible thing? Is this specified anywhere else in the Bible?

6b.   Describe how the two older brothers handled the news of what Ham told them.

7.   Noah knew who had seen him unclothed, and who it was that had protected his drunken condition. Discuss how this was possible.

8.   What impact does this have on our family life today?

9.   Discuss impact and importance of the statement, "Cursed be Canaan". Who made this statement?

~ YOUR THOUGHTS ~

CHAPTER 6

~The Curse of Canaan ~
Part II

Background and Lesson Scriptures:
Genesis 9:18-27; 10:6, 15 - 20; 1 Chronicles 1:8 - 15

"And Ham, the father of Canaan, saw the nakedness of his father...and he[Noah] said, Cursed be Canaan; a servant of servants shall he be unto his brethren." (Genesis 9:22, 25, KJV)

Canaan was the progenitor of the Phoenician people, and the various nations who peopled the seacoast of Palestine. The Hebrew translation of Canaan's name is <u>lowlands.</u> [1] The land of Canaan was described to Moses by the LORD as a land flowing with milk and honey, (Exodus 3:1–8). It was the land that the LORD promised to give his people Israel through Abraham, Isaac, and Jacob years before Moses was born, (Gen 17:1 – 8).

Canaan is located between the Euphrates valley and Egypt, which were the two principal centers of population in the ancient world. It was the geographical center of the Egyptian, Babylonian, Assyrian, Persian, Greek, and Roman cultures. [2] (See map at Appendix A-25).

The 'Curse of Canaan' does not seem fair for one who had nothing to do with the cause of his punishment. We may think: *What an unfortunate, unforgiving, situation for Canaan. How could a loving, forgiving God allow such harsh punishment to fall on an innocent person?*

But then, our thoughts our not God's thoughts, nor our ways His ways, (Isaiah 55:8). This was God's plan; one that would benefit Israel when the time was right for them to inherit the promise God had made to them. They would be gifted all the land of Canaan. Added to that injustice, Canaan was not to be allowed to share the land with Israel; they were to be completely driven out of their homeland and even put to death in many cases. However, Israel didn't exactly follow God's command—they allowed some Canaanites to remain and live in various parts of their country.

The descendants of Canaan included: Sidon/Zidon, Heth, Jebusite, Amorite, Girgasite/Girgashite, Hivite, Arkite, Sinite, Arvadite, Zemarite, and Hamathite. These families are included in the peoples whom God commanded Israel to destroy in later Biblical history.

[1] http://www.blueletterbible.org

[2] Halley's Bible Handbook, Zondervan Publishing House, 1965, pg. 37

The Sanctity of Privacy:
Genesis 9:19 - 23

1.   God knew all about the wine incident with Noah's sons. What could have been His reasoning to allow this to happen?

2.   The curse was upon Ham's son, not upon Ham. What are your thoughts about this?

3.   Research and discuss how and when this curse would start.

4.   What does the phrase <u>servant of servants</u> denote?

Shem Is Blessed:
Genesis 9:26 - 27
5.   Shem was the first son of Noah to receive his father's blessing.
What was Shem's blessing?

6a.   Name the descendants of Shem of today.

6b.   Research and discuss where their city borders are.

7.   Name the descendants of Japheth, and discuss their borders.
(10:25)

The Canaanites:
Genesis 10:6; 15 - 20

8.   Where are the borders of the Canaanites? Give scripture references and find the surrounding areas on a map.

9.   Noah's family populated the earth after the flood. Discuss the division of his family into nations?

10.   Look up the connotation of the word <u>nation</u>. Discuss.

~ YOUR THOUGHTS ~

CHAPTER 7

~ Son of Noah—Shem ~
Part I

Background Reading: Genesis 5: 10-11
Lesson Scriptures: Genesis 10:21-32;
11:10-30; 1 Chronicles 1:1-27

"And he said, Blessed [be] the LORD God of Shem; and Canaan shall be his servant," (Genesis 9:26, KJV).

According to Genesis 5:32, Noah was five hundred years old before he became a father, and he fathered only three sons: Shem, Ham, and Japheth, (Gen 6:10; 9:18-19). These are the men, and their wives, whose responsibility it was to repopulate the earth after the flood, into all generations. Mrs. Noah is never mentioned.

Shem is introduced first in Genesis 9:18, and appears in many other verses. According to some writers and commentators, Japheth seems to be the elder, (Genesis 10:21), yet it is still a matter of interpretation. The first son mentioned in the recording of sons usually tells who the elder son is. Then at times, as in this case, it is hard to decipher. Noah called Ham the younger son, (Gen 9:24).

Noah

This lesson centers primarily on Shem, an ancestor of Abraham and a forefather of Israel. Shem's seed began with Elam, Asshur, Arphaxad, Lud, and Aram. Then after a few hundred years, Arphaxad begat Salah, and Salah begat Eber, who begat Peleg, who begat Reu, who begat Serug; and Serug begat Nahor.

And Nahor begat Terah; the father of Abram/Abraham. Included in this birth line are the births of Sarai, Rebekah, Milcah, Leah, and Rachel. Sarai, later renamed Sarah, was the daughter of Terah, as well as his daughter-in-law—she was married to Terah's son Abram, later renamed Abraham.

The mother of Abram, and the mother of Sarai, is also not mentioned, but scripture relates that Sarai was Abraham's half-sister, (Gen 20:2, 12). Milcah gave birth to eight sons, one of them Bethuel, who was the father of Rebekah. Rebekah married Isaac and was the mother to Esau and Jacob. Jacob, who was renamed Israel, became the father of the twelve tribes.

As stated before, not all offspring are named in the Bible, and I only attempt to explore those who are primary figureheads of our Biblical history.

Genealogy of Shem
Scriptures Genesis 10:21-32
1.   Chart the generations of Shem from these verses.   Research the
Hebrew translation of their names, list their ages where indicated for later
reference and comparison.

Comparative Genealogy of Shem:
Genesis 11:10-26

2.   Chart the descendants of Shem as introduced in these verses. Then compare the genealogy of chapter 11 to the family listed in chapter 10.

In Peleg's Generation:
Look again at Genesis 10:25-32

3.   It is interesting to note that Peleg's name translates as 'division'. Discuss the implication of this prophetic translation.

4.   Joktan, is Peleg's brother. What does his name denote, and which nation is he the ancestor of? Give references.

5.   Find the location on a map where Joktan's people dwelled, and notice the relationship to the proximity to the garden at Eden.   Any insight?

6.   Discuss the name <u>Obal</u> in verse 28—the different pronunciations, and the meaning. Discuss how this name was to be used in a future generation.

7.   Notice in Genesis 10, the genealogies began with those of Japheth. In chapter 11, Shem's families are the only genealogy listed. Discuss the implication of the order of introduction in these families?

~ YOUR THOUGHTS ~

CHAPTER 8

~ Son of Noah—Shem ~
Part II

Background Reading: Genesis 5: 10-11; Genesis 10-11
Lesson Scriptures: 1 Chronicles 1:1-27

"Adam, Sheth, Enosh,...The sons of Japheth;...The sons of Ham;...The sons of Shem;...," (1 Chronicles 1;1, 5, 8, 17; KJV)

The book of Chronicles is closely aligned with the recordings of several books of the Old Testaments. Chronicles is translated in Hebrew as 'Daily Matters,' indicating that the information found in the books of the Chronicles were of primary importance to everything that happened in the lives of Israel's early leaders. The two books of Chronicles originally comprised just one book, and were later divided into two by the Greek translators of the Old Testament. [1]

Chronicles traces the history of Israel from the beginning of humanity to the fall of Jerusalem. The books include a record of details not found in the books of Samuel and Kings. Jewish tradition assigns authorship of these two books to Ezra, whose duties as a priest and a scribe, provide an excellent source of information which helps build his extraordinary background. These experiences lend credibility to Ezra's ability to compile such history as that written in Chronicles, (Ezra 7:11). [2]

The word <u>chronicles</u> is always expressed in Biblical verses as: 'the book of the chronicles of the kings'. Except in four verses. It is an English title, and the Hebrew word associated with it is <u>dabar,</u> and is pronounced as (dä vä'). It projects the following: speech, speaking, an utterance, word or words, business, occupation, acts, something that matters. Jewish tradition also alludes to the fact that Nehemiah had considerable information which his compatriot, Ezra, might gather for writing the two books of Chronicles. [3]

I mention these facts as background. You will find various other revealing facts in different reference materials.

[1]   King James Study Bible, pg 658

[2]   Ibid

[3]   Ibid

Another Generational Version:
Read: 1 Chronicles 1:17-34

1.   Discuss the Hebrew translation of Chronicles.

2.   Draw a comparison chart of Shem's family line as shown in this chapter. List the similarities and differences to Genesis 10 and 11.

3a.   Review the various lists of genealogies found in 1 Chronicles, chapter one. Can you determine anything from the writing there as compared with that of Genesis chapter 10?

3b.   Discuss the people who are direct descendants of Shem as you know them today.

4.   Looking back at Shem's ancestors, how long did Adam live? Seth? Enoch? Methuselah? Lamech? Noah?

5.   What is the meaning of each of these men's names?

Adam_____

Enoch_____

Lamech_____

Methuselah_____

Noah_____

Seth_____

6a.   How long did Noah live before he became father to Shem, Ham, and Japheth?

6b.   The Bible records the ages of certain men as to when they became fathers, and when they died. Why do you think this is relevant?

7.   Discuss Noah's forefather who didn't die a natural death, but was taken by God. Give references.

8.   How many wives did Adam have? Noah? What were their names?

9.   Are you curious about which of Noah's three sons you are a descendant of? How can you find out?

~ YOUR THOUGHTS ~

CHAPTER 9

~ Son of Noah—Shem ~
Part III

Background and Lesson Scriptures:
Genesis 10:21-32; 11:10-26;

"Unto Shem also, the father of all the children of Eber, the brother of Japheth the elder, even to him were children born." (Genesis 10:21; KJV).

Genesis 10 and 11 don't offer much in the way of information other than generations of who's who in the family history of the Bible. However, there is enough to spark a lively discussion of the way in which different verses list the relative insights of each brother's descendants.

For instance, have you ever pondered on why only the birth-line of one's father is given in Biblical family lines? Except in very special cases do we learn the identity of one's mother, or whether there were female children born to a particular patriarch. God, in His infinite wisdom, was leaving trails for us discover, and foretelling our future.

Modern science has confirmed that the study of DNA can prove the lineage of a man, and that of his sister/s, from the bloodline or DNA of their father or brother. However, the ancestry of one's mother can only be proven from the DNA of one's mother, sister, or daughter.

What is DNA? The technical, scientific name is Deoxyribonucleic Acid, which is an acid found in the nucleus of our cells that maps our biological being, making us uniquely different, by a certain degree of cell characteristics, from any and every other human being on earth. [1]

Is Science proving the Bible, or is the Bible foretelling of Science?

[1] http://www.ehow.com

Shem, Japheth, Eber:
Read: Genesis 10:21-32

1.   Look at how the facts are introduced in verse 21. Is there a noteworthy fiber?

2.   Shem is recorded as the brother of Japheth in this passage. Ham is not. Discuss.

2.   Of what importance did a son of Eber have toward the national development of the family's future? Define and discuss.

3.   Research and discuss how the earth was divided in verse 25.

4.   The descendants of Joktan lived in an area bordered by Mesha, and mountains on the east. What is the translation of the town's name, and the surrounding mountain terrain?

5a.   How were the sons of Shem divided? (verses 31 and 32).

5b.   Discover what is said of Shem's family in verses 31 and 32?

6.   Research who else, in the ancestry of Shem and his brothers, lived in the east country? Give references and discuss.

Family History:
Genesis 11:10-26

7.   Who was Shem's son Arphaxad? When was he born, and how old was Shem at his birth?

8.   Chart the sons of Shem through the descendants of Terah.

9. Who was the most famous son of Terah? Discuss his role in history.

~ YOUR THOUGHTS ~

CHAPTER 10

~ Son of Noah—Japheth ~

Background and Lesson Scriptures:
Genesis 10:2-5; 1 Chronicles 1:5-7

"God shall enlarge Japheth, and he shall dwell in the tents of Shem; and Canaan shall be his servant, (Genesis 9:27, KJV)."

Very little is said about Japheth in introducing Noah's sons. The Bible does say that God would enlarge the house of Japheth, which indicates several possibilities. One translation is to be made spacious, wide or open. Japheth's descendants and their influence could become widespread. They could also be blessed economically, financially, as well as with many sons and daughters. Japheth and his family of seven sons, including wives and children, shared the camps of his brother Shem. Their nephew Canaan and all his line were servants of Shem and Japheth.

Hopefully, this lesson will stimulate your interest in a sparsely discussed son of Noah, and give you a broader knowledge about Japheth's place in Biblical history. Every insight builds on the legacy and appreciation of how Japheth's family impacted the world.

Noah

Descendants of Japheth
Read: Genesis 10:2-5
1. Trace the Japheth family line.

Japheth

Gomer	Magog	Madai	Javan

Tubal	Meshech	Tiras

2.   List the Hebrew translation of the names of each son and grandson of Japheth, and trace the cities that are associated with their lands. Discuss their importance.

Japheth

_____

_____

_____

_____

_____

_____

_____

_____

Noah

_____

_____

_____

_____

_____

_____

_____

3a.   Explain the isles of the Gentiles in verse five?

3b.   How do these isles relate to Gentiles in other Bible verses?

4.   What is the meaning of <u>isles</u> in verse 5?

5.   Can you determine how and when the land was divided among the nations? Give references and discuss.

Family of Gentiles:
Genesis 10:20-32
6.   Discuss the meaning of how tongue/tongues is used in verse 20. Give references.

7.   Compare the words of 10:5 with that of 10:20 and 10:31. Discuss the use of <u>Gentiles</u> in relation to Japheth's family and not his two brothers.

Chronicle of Noah's Sons
1 Chronicles 1:5-7
8.   Compare the verses in 1 Chronicles 1:5-7 to those in Genesis. What differences, if any, do you observe?

9.   Magog appears five times in the whole Bible and is associated with another name. Research the verses and discuss the implications.

10.   Japheth's son Javan, was also the forefather of a country.   Name the country, and the references that point to this fact.

11.   Names are often repeated in the Bible with sons being named after their fathers, their father's brothers, their grandfathers, etc.   One of Shem's grandsons had the same name as one of Japheth's sons.   Who was he? What was the alternate pronunciation?   (See 10:2 & 23).

~ YOUR THOUGHTS ~

CHAPTER 11

~ A Tower To Heaven ~

Background Reading: Genesis 10
Lesson Scripture: Genesis 11:2 - 5

"And they said,…, let us build us a city and a tower, whose top [may reach] unto heaven; and let us make us a name, lest we be scattered abroad upon the face of the whole earth." (Gen 11:4, KJV).

Throughout history, men have been fascinated with obtaining height—building towers; the tallest buildings, climbing the tallest mountain peak, constructing high crescent bridges, and flying into the heavens. Is it because men want to be closer to heaven? Or, a desire to build something that soars higher than another building? Or above everything else? Or, is it a human trait to be elevated above others? Or, is it just plain curious ingenuity?

In verse four of Genesis eleven, a thought is introduced that the people wanted to build so that their building's height would reach into heaven. God interpreted their thoughts as indicative of wanting to know more than He was ready for man to know. Any imagination of man's heart could and would be accomplished; nothing would be restrained from them, if they set their mind to do and have it.

The building of this tower was in the plain of Shinar, which is defined as being a country of two rivers. It was also the ancient name of the territory of Babylonia or Chaldea.[1] Babylonia was situated at the mouth of the Euphrates and Tigris rivers; and for many centuries was the center of a dense population. The timeframe of construction occurred in the fourth generation after the Flood, during the time of the birth of Peleg, which was 101 years after the Flood—according to Halley's Bible Handbook. [2]

The tower was eventually completed and became a pattern for other towers built in Babylonian cities. It may even have been the example used to design the building of the Pyramids of Egypt. An archaeologist (G. Smith) found an ancient tablet among ruins in Babylon that read, "The building of this illustrious tower offended the gods. In a night they threw down what they had built. They scattered them abroad, and made strange their speech." [3]

However, it was not 'the gods' that were offended; it was the 'God'.

[1] www.blueletterbible.org

[2] Henry H. Halley, *Halley's Bible Handbook*, 24th ed., p. 82

[3] ibid, p. 84

Into A New Land:
Read: Genesis 11:2 - 5

1.   Explain the meaning of 'the whole earth' at the time of this story.

2.   There was a universal language during this time. What was it?
Explain the reasoning for your answer.

3a.   Who were the people who journeyed in verse two? Why would
these families leave their homes to find another place to live?

3b.   If they traveled from the east, where were they coming from?

4.   Discuss the location of the land Shinar, where these families finally decided to settle. Research what the places are called today.

Leaving A Legacy:
Genesis 4
5.   Name the rivers that ran through the land.

6.   Wanting to make a name for yourself seems to be a common human trait. What could have been the deciding force behind the desire of these families to make a name for themselves?

7.   The people thought they eventually might be scattered into all parts of the earth. How do you suppose they came to that conclusion?

8.   Doesn't the LORD have fore-knowledge of anything that man might think even before man himself knows what he's thinking? Expound on this.

Come Let Us Go Down:
Genesis 11:5
9.   After building their communities, the men wanted to start another project. Discuss.

10.   God spoke in verse six. Was He talking to himself? What was his concern?

11.   The phrase <u>go to</u> actually translates as <u>come let us.</u> Discuss the context of this conversation.

12.   Discuss God's decision to take countermeasures against the construction of this tower.

CHAPTER 12

~ New Languages ~
A Division Of Speech

Background Reading: Genesis 10
Lesson Scriptures: Genesis 11:1, 6 - 9

"And the whole earth was of one language, ...let us go down, and there confound their language, that they may not understand one another's speech."
(Genesis 11:1 & 7; KJV).

Genesis chapter eleven is the passage where we find the first division of languages. Language is interpreted as tongues, and vice versa. This is substantiated by the 'Law of First Mention'. Verse thirty-one of Genesis chapter ten describes the generations of Noah's sons and family lines distinguished *after their tongues*.

Therefore to speak in a particular tongue means to speak in a different language. One form of speech is often unfamiliar to people who don't speak that same language. It is the basic differentiation that distinguishes one nationality of people from another. Before this time, all peoples of the earth spoke the same language. The separation of tongues or languages came after the events in chapter eleven when the tower of Babel was constructed.

Noah

According to Halley's Bible Handbook, the confusion of tongues happened about the time of the birth of Peleg, whose ancestors were Shem and Noah.[1] Genesis 10:25 states that in the day of Peleg, the earth was divided, signifying that the division happened during Peleg's lifetime.

The subject of tongues is a controversial one among different religions. I will not attempt to determine the uttering of different tongues in this writing. This lesson concentrates on the events of chapter eleven where God divided his people who were so ambitious they wanted to make a name for themselves. One effective way to divide and confuse was to cause them to speak different languages or tongues.

[1] Henry H. Halley, *Halley's Bible Handbook*, 24th ed., p. 83.

The Language Factors
Genesis 11:1—6
1.   Do you speak more than one language? Name them, and give examples of a few simple words or phrases, along with their interpretation.

2.   If there is a difference between the words *language* and *speech*, explain what it is.

The Division of Languages
Genesis 11:7-9
3.   Again God says, "Let us…;" what is the significance of these words? Research where these words have occurred previously.

4.   Discuss the meaning of God's words "let us go down".

The LORD Comes Down
Genesis 11:5

5a.   In verse seven the LORD says, "let us go down. Explain the importance of this invitation and events.

5b.   Is there a difference in the LORD coming down in verse five and the 'let us' go down in verse seven?

6a.   Not only did God confuse the language of the people, He did something else. Discuss. (v8)

6b.   Define Diaspora. How was this accomplished?

7.   After the people were scattered, what happened to the city and tower?

8.   The place where they had begun to build had a new name. What was it called, and what is its meaning?

9.   Where is Babylon located today?

10.   Have you noticed a change in the way you talk and act as you grow in your knowledge of God's Word? Discuss.

~ Speech Representation ~

And so now it was fixed; official.
God had determined that
from that moment forward
One family of people, and their descendants,
Would not, could not
readily know, or interpret
The dialect spoken by another.

Until, of course, there was a
Proper time, and means to study
Identification of,
Evidence of,
Friend…maybe; or Foe…perhaps.

Family connections, maybe…
Or…, Err…, And…,
Friendly non-verbal approach, with
Uh…, And…,
No threatening demeanor,
And…, ah…,
Little evidence of hidden motivation.

Then maybe, just maybe,
Now, we can communicate.
By means other than speech, until…
We understand the Patterns
of Identification, of what
is what, And who…
is who… and How…
We go from… Where we are…
To… where we want
To be.

---

tjjohnson, April 2010

~ YOUR THOUGHTS '~

GENEALOGY

REFERENCE TABLES

APPENDIX A

I
GOD

Name	Translation	Nation/s
GOD Elōhīym (el-o-heem')	The Godhead, Rulers, Judges	A plural of Majesty with a singular verb
Adam (aw-dawm')	Man, mankind	First man; father of humankind
Eve (khav-vaw') Woman (ish-shaw')	Life or living; Taken out of man	First woman; mother of humankind; called Woman, and then Eve

All References in Bibliography:

II
Adam

Name	Translation	Nation/s
Adam (aw-dawm') & **Eve** begat:	Man, mankind	First man; father of humankind; lived to be 930 yrs old
a. Cain (kah'-yin)	Acquire; Possession	Tiller of the ground; killed his brother because of envy, Gen 4:1-8
b. Abel (heh'-bel)	Breath; Keeper	Keeper of sheep
c. Seth (shayth)	Appointed; Compensation	Seth lived to be 912 yrs old; Adam 130 at Seth's birth. Gen 4:25; 5:3
d. Other sons & daughters		Gen 5:4

II-a: Cain
(Gen 4:16-18)

Name	Translation	Nation/s
Cain begat: (kah'-yin)	Acquire; Possession	Tiller of the ground; killed his brother because of envy, Gen 4:1-8
Enoch (khan-oke')	Dedicated, Initiated	Cain built a city named after Enoch (Gen 4:17)

II-a: Cain; Enoch

Name	Translation	Nation/s
Enoch begat: (khan-oke')	Dedicated, Initiated	Cain built a city named after Enoch (Gen 4:17)
Irad (ee-rawd')		

II-a: Cain; Enoch; Irad

Name	Translation	Nation/s
Irad begat: (ee-rawd')		(Gen 4:18)
1. Mehujael (mekh-oo-yaw-ale')	Smitten by God	

II-a: Cain; Enoch; Irad; Mehujael

Name	Translation	Nation/s
Mehujael begat: (mekh-oo-yaw-ale')		(Gen 4:18)
1. Methusael (meth-oo-shaw-ale')	Who is of God	

II-a: Cain; Enoch; Irad; Mehujael; Methusael

Name	Translation	Nation/s
Methusael (mcth-oo-shaw-alc')	Who is of God	(Gen 4:18)
1. Lamech (leh'-mek)	Powerful	

II-a: Cain; Enoch; Irad; Mehujael; Methusael; Lamech

Name	Translation	Nation/s
Lamech begat: **& Adah** (aw-daw')	Powerful Ornament	Genesis 4:19-22
1. Jabal (yaw-bawl')		Father of tent dwellers, and livestock owners
2. Jubal (yoo-bawl')		Father of harp and flute musicians

II-a: Lamech & wife Zillah
Cain; Enoch; Irad; Mehujael; Methusael; Lamech

Name	Translation	Nation/s
Lamech & **Zillah begat:** (tsil-law')	Powerful/ Shade	(Gen 4:22)
1. **Tubal-cain** (too-bal' kah'-yin)	Thou will be brought of Cain	Craftsman in brass and iron
2. **Naamah** (nah-am-aw')	Loveliness	A daughter

II-c: Adam; Seth

Name	Translation	Nation/s
c. **Seth** begat: (shayth)	Appointed; Compensation	Lived to be 912 yrs old Begat other sons and daughters
Enos (Ē'nŏs)	A man	Seth, 105 at birth of Enos (Gen 5:6)

II-c: Adam; Seth; Enos

Name	Translation	Nation/s
Enos begat: (Ē'nŏs)	A man	Lived to be 905 yrs old Begat other sons and daughters
Cainan (kay-nawn')	Possession	Enos, 90 at birth of Cainan (Gen 5:9)

II-c: Adam; Seth; Enos; Cainan
(Gen 5:12-29)

Name	Translation	Nation/s
Cainan begat: (kay-nawn')	Possession	Lived to be 910 yrs old: Begat other children
Mahalaleel (mah-hal-al-ale')	Praise of God	70 at birth of Mahalaleel (Gen 5:12)

II-c: Adam; Seth; Enos; Cainan; Mahalaleel

Name	Translation	Nation/s
Mahalaleel (mah-hal-al-ale')	Praise of God	Lived to be 895 yrs old: Begat other children
Jared (yeh'-red)	Descent	65 at Jared's birth (Gen 5:15)

II-c: Adam; Seth; Enos; Cainan; Mahalaleel; Jared

Name	Translation	Nation/s
Jared begat: (yeh'-red)	Descent	Lived to be 962 yrs old: Begat other sons and daughters
Enoch khan-oke')	Dedicated, Initiated	162 at birth of Enoch. (Gen 5:18)

II-c: Adam; Seth; Enos; Cainan; Mahalaleel; Jared; Enoch

Name	Translation	Nation/s
Enoch begat: (khan-oke')	Dedicated	365 yrs when God took him, (Gen 5:24); had other sons and daughters
Methuselah (meth-oo-sheh'-lakh)	Man of the javelin	65 at Methuselah's birth (Gen 5:21)

II-c: Adam; Seth; Enos; Cainan; Mahalaleel; Jared; Enoch; Methuselah

Name	Translation	Nation/s
Methuselah (meth-oo-sheh'-lakh)	Man of the javelin	Lived 969 yrs; oldest man; Begat other sons and daughters
Lamech (leh'-mek)	Powerful	187 at Lamech's birth (Gen 5:25)

Adam; Seth; Enos; Cainan; Mahalaleel; Jared; Enoch; II-c: Methuselah; Lamech

Name	Translation	Nation/s
Lamech begat: (leh'-mek)	Powerful	777 yrs at death; 182 at birth of Noah. Begat other sons and daughters
Noah** (nō'å)/noē	Rest or comfort	He shall comfort us concerning our work & toil of the ground; Gen 5:29

III. Noah's Sons
Adam; Seth; Enos; Cainan; Mahalaleel; Jared;
Enoch; Methuselah; Lamech; Noah
(Gen 5:29-32; 6:9-10, 18-19; 10:2-25; 11:10-32)

Name	Translation	Nation/s
Noah begat: (nō'ả)	Rest or comfort	Found grace in the eyes of God; age 500 at birth of Shem; Gen 5:32
a. Shem (shěm)	Name, renown	Father of Semitic tribes
b. Ham (hăm)	Hot	Father of Canaanites; collective name for Egyptians; Ethiopia, Libya
c. Japheth (jā' feth)	Opened, God will enlarge	Coastline peoples; went North to Europe & Asia

III-b: Noah; Ham
(Gen 10:6)

Name	Translation	Nation/s
Ham begat: (hăm)	Hot	Father of Canaanites; collective name for Egyptians; Ethiopia, Libya
1. Cush (koosh)	Black	Grandson of Noah; progenitor of the southernmost peoples of Africa, near the Nile (Ethiopia):Ez 38:5
2. Mizraim (mits-rah'-yim)	Land of the Copts	Northeastern section of Africa, adjacent to Palestine, and through which the Nile flows; natives of Egypt
3. Phut/Put (poot)	A Bow	People of Libya; Ezk 38:5
4. Canaan (ken-ah'-an)	Lowland	Progenitor of the Phoenicians and the seacoast of Palestine

III-b1: Noah; Ham; Cush
(Gen 10:6-8)

Name	Translation	Nation/s
Cush begat: (koosh)	Black	Grandson of Noah; pro-genitor of the southernmost peoples located in Africa, near the Nile (Ethiopia); Gen 10:6-8
a. Seba (seb-aw')	Drink thou	A nation south of Palestine
b. Havilah (khav-ee-law')	Circle	District in Arabia of the Ishmaelite named from the 2nd son of Cush;
c. Sabtah (sab-taw')	Unknown	
d. Raamah (rah-maw')	Horse's mane	
e. Sabtechan (sab-tē-aw')	Striking	
f. Nimrod (nim-rode')	Let us revolt; valiant, rebel	He was a rebel leader, revolted before the Lord; Babel was the beginning of his kingdoms, Gen 11:1-9.

III-b1(d): Noah; Ham; Cush; Ramaah

Name	Translation	Nation/s
Raamah: (rah-maw')	Horse's mane	(Gen 10:7)
1. Sheba (sheb-aw')	Seven; an oath	Arabian people of northwest part of Persian Gulf.
2. Dedan (ded-awn')	Low country	

III-b1(f): Nimrod's Kingdoms
Noah; Ham; Cush; Nimrod
(Gen 10:8-12)

Name	Translation	Nation/s
Nimrod begat:		Cities built by sons of Nimrod.
1. Babel (baw-bel')	Confusion by mixing	Ancient site and/or capital of Babylonia (modern Hillah) situated on the Euphrates.
2. Erech (eh'-rek)	Long	City 40 miles (64 km) northwest of Ur toward Babylon on the left bank of the Euphrates river.
3. Accad (ak-kad')	Stubble	City of north Babylonia, also the district around it.
4. Calneh (kal-neh')	Fortress of Anu	In the land of Shinar. ancient Babylonia or Chaldea; country of two rivers
5. Nineveh (nee-nev-ay')	Abode of Ninus	In the land of Assyria (2Ki 19:36; Micah 5:6)
6. Rehoboth (rekh-o-both')	Wide places	Also Rehoboth-IR
7. Calah (keh'-lakh)	Vigor	Capital of the ancient kingdom of Assyria; located on the east bank of the Tigris river
8. Resen (reh'-sen)	Bridle	In Assyria between Nineveh and Calah

III-b2: Noah; Ham; Mizraim
(Gen 10:13; 1Chr. 1:8-12)

Name	Translation	Nation/s
Mizraim: (mits-rah'-yim)	Egypt; land of the Copts	Country, northeast of Africa, adjacent to Palestine; where the Nile flows. Egyptian
a. Ludim (loo-dee')	Travailings	
b. Anamim (an-aw-meem')	Affliction of the waters	
c. Lehabim (leh-haw-beem')	Flames	
d. Naphtuhim (naf-too-kheem)	Openings	
e. Pathrusim (path-roo-see')		See Pathros, south region
f. Casluhim (kas-loo'-kheem)	Fortified	Progenitors of the Philistines and Caphtorim
g. Caphtorim (kaf-to-ree')	Caphtor, crown	Cretans as the inhabitants of Caphtor, distinct from Philistines

III- b2(f): Noah; Ham; Mizraim; Casluhim
(Gen 10:4; 1Chr. 1:12)

Name	Translation	Nation/s
Casluhim: (kas-loo'-kheem)	Fortified	Progenitors of the Philistines and Caphtorim
1. Philistim (pel-ish-tee')	Immigrants; Can be person, or city	Inhabitant of Philistia; descendants of Mizraim who immigrated from Caphtor to west seacoast of Canaan

III-b4: Noah; Ham; Canaan
(Gen 10:15-19; 1Chr. 1:13-16)

Name	Translation	Nation/s
Canaan begat: (ken-ah'-an)	Lowland	4th son of Ham; progenitor of the Phoenicians and various nations who peopled the seacoast of Palestine
a. Sidon/Zidon (tsee-done')	Hunting	Ancient Phoenician city, on Mediterranean, north of Tyre
b. Heth (khayth)	Terror	Progenitor of the Hittites
c. Jebus/ Jubsite (yeb-oo-see')	Descendants of Jebus	Lived in or around the site of Jebus, early name for Jerusalem
d. Amorite (em-o-ree')	A sayer	Of east Canaan and beyond the Jordan, ousted by the Israelite incursion from Egypt
e. Girgasite/ Girgashite (ghir-gaw-shee')	Dwells on clay soil	Living east of the sea of Galilee when the Israelites entered the promised land
f. Hivite (khiv-vee')	Villagers	Living in northern Canaan near Mount Hermon at the time of the conquest
g. Arkite (ar-kee')	Gnawing	Inhabitant of Arki or Arka
h. Sinite (see-nee')	Thorn or Clay	Inhabiting the northern part of the Lebanon district
i. Arvadite (ar-vaw-dee')	I shall break loose	
j. Zemarite (tsem-aw-ree')		
k. Hamathite (kham-aw-thee')	Fortress[3]	Ancient capital city of upper Syria.

III-c: Noah; Japheth
(Gen 10:2-5; 1Chr. 1:5-7)

Name	Translation	Nation/s
Japheth begat: (jā' feth)	Opened, God will enlarge	Coastline peoples; went North to Europe & Asia
1. **Gomer** (go'-mer)	Complete	Progenitor of early Cimmerians and other Celtic families
2. **Magog** (maw-gogue')	Land of Gog	Progenitor of Scythians, Lydians, Tartars of Russia
3. **Madai** (maw-dah'-ee)	Media, Middle lands	Known as Medes, same area as modern Iran
4. **Javan** (yaw-vawn')	Ionia or Greece	Inhabitants of Greece, Syria*
5. **Tubal** (too-bal')	He shall be brought	A region of eastern Asia Minor' S. Black Sea, Spain*
6. **Meshech** (meh'-shek)	Drawing out; tall	Thought to be progenitors of Russians and other Slavics peoples.
7. **Tiras** (tee-rawce')	Desire	Thracians*

III-c1: Noah; Japheth; Gomer

Name	Translation	Nation/s
Gomer begat: (go'-mer)	Complete	Progenitor of the early Cimmerians and other branches of the Celtics
a. **Ashkenaz** (ash-ken-az')	A man sprinkled; scattered fire	Assyrians, Scythians[3] ; Associated with Ararat (Jer 51:27)
b. **Riphath** (ree-fath')	Spoken	
c. **Togarmah** (to-gar-maw')	Thou will break her	Of the far north (Ez 38:2); followers of Gog

*Good Things Company, Norman, OK, 1975. 14 Printing

III-a: Noah; Shem
(Gen 10:21-22; 1Chr. 1:17)

Name	Translation	Nation/s
Shem begat: (shĕm)	Name, renown	Father of Semitic tribes lived to be 500 yrs old
1. Elam (ē' lăm)	Eternity	
2. Asshur (ăsh' ûr)	Step	Assyria; built Nineveh, Rehoboth, Calah, Resen (Gen 10:11)
3. Arphaxad (är-făx' ăd); 2479 BC		Forefather of Abraham, and many other sons and daughters (Gen 11:11)
4. Lud (lŭd)	Strife	Of the people of Lydia in Asia Minor; Northern Africa
5. Aram (ă'răm)	Exalted; means Syria, also Mesopotamia (Judges 3:10; 3:6)	Arameans of Phoenicia, Syria is short for Assyria; Mesopotamia; Seleucid; Aramaic; Rebekah's ancestry (Gen 25:20; Deu 26:5)

III-a3: Noah; Shem; Arphaxad
(Gen 10:24; 1Chr. 1:18)

Name	Translation	Nation/s
Arphaxad: (är-făx' ăd)		Lived 438 yrs ancestor of Abraham
Salah/ Shelah (sā' lă)	Missile, javelin, (or Shelah) or sprout	Shelach {sheh'-lakh}

III-a3: Noah; Shem; Arphaxad; Salah
(Gen 10:24; 11:14; 1Chr. 1:18)

Name	Translation	Nation/s
Salah begat: (sā' lȧ)		Lived 433 yrs other sons and daughters
1. Eber , Heber, or Ebet (ē' bêr)	Region beyond the river	Said to be the founder of Hebrews

III-a3: Noah; Shem; Arphaxad; Salah; Eber
(Gen 10:25; 11:16; 1Chr. 1:19)

Name	Translation	Nation/s
Eber begat:	Region beyond; immigrant	Lived 464 yrs; other sons and daughters
a. Peleg (pē' lĕg)	Division	In his day the earth was divided
b. Joktan (jŏk' tăn)	Smallness	Patriarch of Arabia

III-a3: Noah; Shem; Arphaxad; Salah; Eber; Peleg
(Gen 11:18; 1Chr. 1:4-27)

Name	Translation	Nation/s
Peleg begat: (pē' lĕg)	Division	Lived 239 yrs; other sons and daughters
1. Reu (rē' ū)	Friendship	Called Ragau in Luke 3:35

III-a3: Noah; Shem; Arphaxad; Salah; Eber; Peleg; Reu
(Gen 11:20-24; 1Chr. 1:24-27)

Name	Translation	Nation/s
Reu begat: (rē' ū)	Friendship	Lived 239 yrs; other sons and daughters
a. Serug (sē'rŭg)	Shoot or tendril	Called Saruch in Lu 3:35, city in Mesopotania, near Haran

III-a3: Noah; Shem; Arphaxad; Salah; Eber; Peleg; Reu; Serug

Name	Translation	Nation/s
Serug begat: (sē'rŭg)		Lived 230 yrs; other sons and daughters; Gen 11:22
1. Nahor (nā' hôr)	Snorting	

III-a3: Noah; Shem; Arphaxad; Salah; Eber; Peleg; Reu; Serug; Nahor

Name	Translation	Nation/s
Nahor begat: (nā' hôr)	Snorting	Lived 148 yrs; other sons and daughters; Gen 11:24
a. Terah (tē'rá)	Station Terach (teh'-rakh)	

IV: Noah; Shem; ... Terah;
& Abram's Mother

(Gen 10:31; 11:26-29; 22:20-24)

Name	Translation	Nation/s
Terah begat: (tē' rȧ)	Terach (teh'-rakh);	205 yrs at birth of Abram
a. Abram (ā' brăm)	Also Abraham, exalted father, high father	Progenitor of **Israel** Father of many Nations
b. Nahor (nā' hôr)	Snorting	Named after his grandfather
c. Haran (hā' răn)	Mountaineer; Father of Lot, Milcah & Iscah	Born in Ur of the Chaldees, land of Haran; his daughter (Milcah) married his brother Nahor

IV: Noah; Shem; ... Terah;
& Sarai's Mother

Name	Translation	Nation/s
Terah begat: (tē'rȧ)	Terach (teh'-rakh);	Father of Abraham
Sarai (sâr' ȧ)	Princess	Abram's half-sister; later changed to Sarah
Others:		Unnamed

III-a3: Noah; Shem; Arphaxad; Salah; Eber; Joktan
(Gen 10:26-30)

Name	Translation	Nation/s
Joktan begat: (yok-tawn') 2nd son of Eber	Smallness	Patriarch of Arabia great-grand of Shem, *Gen 10:26-32*
1. Almodad,	Not measured	(al-mo-dawd')
2. Sheleph	Drawing forth	(sheh'-lef)
3. Hazar-maveth	Village of death	(khats-ar-maw'-veth), of southern Arabia
4. Jerah (yeh'-rakh)	New moon	progenitor of Arabia
5. Hadoram	Noble honor	(had-o-rawm')
6. Uzal	I shall be flooded	(oo-zawl')
7. Diklah	Palm grove	(dik-law')
8. Obal/Ebal	Stripped bare	(o-bawl')
9. Abimael	My father is El (God)	(ab-ee-maw-ale')
10. Sheba, (sheb-aw')	Seven (or an oath)	Also the name of a son of Cush, grandson of Ham
11. Ophir, (o-feer')	Reducing to ashes	Of fine gold; city of southern Arabia where Solomon traded gold
12. Havilah (hăv' ĭ-lá)	Sand land; circle	(khav-ee-law'); city where the Pison river flowed from Eden; the name of a son of Cush and grandson of Ham
13. Jobab (jō'băb)	Howler, calls loudly	Arabian descendants of Joktan; from Mesha (freedom) to Sephar (numbering)

III-a3: Noah; Shem; Aram
(Gen 10:23; 1Chr. 1:17)

Name	Translation	Nation/s
Aram: (ă'răm) *5th son of Shem*	Exalted, Syria	Aramaic, progenitor of Armenian people
Uz (ŭz)	Wooded	Country of Job (Job 1:1); near Edom, Egypt, Moab, Philistia (Jer 25:20)
Hul (hŭl)	Circle	
Gether (gē-'thĕr)	Fear	
Mash (măsh) or Meshech	Drawn out	Also pronounced Meshech (mē'shĕk)

IV-a: Noah; Shem; ... Terah; <u>Abraham</u> & <u>Hagar</u>
(Age 86; Gen 16:15-16; 1Chr. 1:28)

Name	Translation	Nation/s
a. Abram: (ab·răm') & ***Hagar*** begat:	Exalted father; Flight	Name chg to Abraham (Gen 17:5); Hagar—Sarai's Egyptian maid
1. Ishmael (ĭsh' mā-ĕl)	God hears	Forefather of Havilah people & Shur, Egypt toward Assyria

IV-a: Noah; Shem; ... Terah; <u>Abraham</u> & <u>Sarah</u>
(Age 100/Sarah 99; Gen 21:5, 17:17; 1Chr. 1:28)

(Name	Translation	Nation/s
a. <u>**Abraham:**</u> & <u>**Sarah**</u> begat	Father of a multitude; & noblewoman	**Ancestor of Israel;** Sarai now called Sarah; Gen 17:15
2. Isaac (ĭ' zăk)	One laughs	**Forefather of Israel;** Gen 21:1-3

IV-a2: Noah; Shem; ... Terah; Abraham; <u>Isaac</u>
& <u>Rebekah</u>

Name	Translation	Nation/s
<u>**Isaac**</u> (ĭ' zăk) & <u>**Rebekah:**</u>	One laughs; And ensnarer	Age 60 at twins birth; Gen 25:20, 26
1a. Esau (ē'saw)(ā säv')	Hairy/ Red	Of the **Arab** peoples; Forefather of Edom
1b. Jacob * (jă' kūb)	Supplanter/deceit- ful /or heel holder	**Name changed to Israel;** **Father of Israel; Gen 35:10**

*Father of 12 Tribes of Israel

IV-b: Noah; Shem; ... Terah;
Nahor & Milcah
(Gen 22:20-24)

Name	Translation	Nation/s
b. **Nahor** **& Milcah:**	Snorting & Queen	Bro. of Abram & Haran; Milcah, daughter of Haran
1. Huz, (oots)	Wooded	
2. Buz, (booz)	Contempt	
3. Kemuel (kem-oo-ale)	Raised of God	Father of Aram; Gen 22:21
4. Chesed (keh'sed)	Increase	
5. Hazo, (khaz-o')	Vision	
6. Pildash (pil-dawsh')	Flame or fire	
7. Jidlaph (yid-lawf')	Weeping	
8. Bethuel (beth-oo-ale')	Abode of God	Syrian of Padanaram; **father of Rebekah** (See page A-23)

IV-b: Noah; Shem; ... Terah;
Nahor & Reumah

Name	Translation	Nation/s
Nahor & Reumah:	Snorting & elevated	Gen 22:24; Reuman (reh-oo-maw') concubine of Nahor
1. **Tebah**	Slaughter	(teh'-bakh)
2. **Gaham**	Burning	(gah'-kham)
3. **Thahash**	Dugong	(takh'-ash)
4. **Maachah**	Oppression	(mah-ak-aw')

IV-c: Noah; Shem; ... Terah; Nahor; Haran
(Gen 11:27-29)

Name	Translation	Nation/s
c. Haran begat: (hā' răn) Gen 11:29, 31	Mountaineer	Born in Ur of the Chaldees; land of Haran; brother of Nahor & Abram
1. Lot (lŏt)	Covering; envelope	Small bits of wood, pebble, in deciding an issue; followed Abram from Ur
2. Milcah	Queen; (mil-kaw')	(a daughter) Married her uncle, Nahor
3. Iscah	One who looks forth; (yis-kaw')	(a daughter) Gen 11:29

IV-c: Noah; Shem;
... Terah; Nahor; Lot
(Gen 19:30-38)

Name	Translation	Nation/s
Lot & wife:	Covering; (lŏt)	
daughter #1		Heirs to their father lineage
daughter #2		
#1 begat Moab	Of his father	Moabites
#2 begat Ben-ammi	Son of my people	Ammonites

IV-b(8): Noah; Shem; ... Terah;
Nahor & Milcah; Bethuel
(Gen 11:29; 22:20-23; 24:15, 24, 29, 47)

Name	Translation	Nation/s
2h. Bethuel: (bë-thū' ël) (beth-oo-ale)	Abode of God	Syrian of Padanaram
1. Rebekah * (rib-kaw')	Ensnarer	Sister of Laban, **wife of Isaac**, mother of Esau and Jacob
2. Laban, (law-bawn')	White	Father of Leah & Rachel who were wives of Jacob; Gen 29:16; Gen 24:29

IV-b(8): Noah; Shem; ... Terah;
Nahor & Milcah; Bethuel; Laban
(Gen 29:15-30)

Name	Translation	Nation/s
Laban & wife: begat: Gen 29:16	White	Syrian of Padanaram
a. Leah * (lay-aw')	Weary, soft & delicate	**1st wife of Jacob;** mother of Reuben, Simeon, Levi, Judah, Issachar, Zebulun, and Dinah
b. Rachel * (raw-khale)	Ewe, beauty in looks and form	**2nd wife of Jacob;** mother of Joseph, and Benjamin

~ YOUR THOUGHTS ~